COLORADO ROCKIES

BY ANTHONY K. HEWSON

An Imprint of Abdo Publishing
abdobooks.com

abdobooks.com

Published by Abdo Publishing, a division of ABDO, PO Box 398166, Minneapolis, Minnesota 55439.

Printed in China.
102022
012023

Cover Photo: Justin Edmonds/Getty Images Sport/Getty Images
Interior Photos: Stacy Revere/Getty Images Sport/Getty Images, 4; Mitchell Layton/Getty Images Sport/Getty Images, 6, 8; Ronald C. Modra/Getty Images Sport/Getty Images, 9; Focus on Sport/Getty Images Sport/Getty Images, 11, 12, 16; Stephen Dunn/Allsport/Getty Images Sport/Getty Images, 14; Larry Goren/Four Seam Images/AP Images, 19; David Zalubowski/AP Images, 21, 28; Doug Pensinger/Getty Images Sport/Getty Images, 22, 27, 35; Chris Carlson/AP Images, 25; Getty Images Sport/Getty Images, 31; Victor Decolongon/Getty Images Sport/Getty Images, 32; Karl Gehring/Denver Post/Getty Images, 36; Pouya Dianat/Atlanta Braves/Getty Images Sport/Getty Images, 37; Rob Leiter/MLB/Getty Images Sport/Getty Images, 38; Mitchell Leff/Getty Images Sport/Getty Images, 41

Editor: Charlie Beattie
Series Designer: Becky Daum

Library of Congress Control Number: 2022940482

Publisher's Cataloging-in-Publication Data

Names: Hewson, Anthony K., author.
Title: Colorado Rockies / by Anthony K. Hewson
Description: Minneapolis, Minnesota: Abdo Publishing, 2023 | Series: Inside MLB | Includes online resources and index.
Identifiers: ISBN 9781098290160 (lib. bdg.) | ISBN 9781098275365 (ebook)
Subjects: LCSH: Colorado Rockies (Baseball team)--Juvenile literature. | Baseball teams--Juvenile literature. | Professional sports--Juvenile literature. | Sports franchises--Juvenile literature. | Major League Baseball (Organization)--Juvenile literature.
Classification: DDC 796.35764--dc23

TABLE OF

CONTENTS

CHAPTER 1

MILE HIGH BASEBALL

Tony Wolters was not the Colorado Rockies' first choice to bat in a key playoff situation. The team's third-string catcher had hit just .170 during the regular season. But in the 13th inning of the 2018 National League (NL) wild-card game, the Rockies were running out of players.

Wolters stepped into the Wrigley Field batter's box to face the Chicago Cubs' Kyle Hendricks. Runners were on first and third. Hendricks quickly took control, using his signature changeup to put Wolters down 0–2 in the count. Wolters worked the count to 1–2 on a fastball.

Hendricks tried another changeup. This time Wolters was ready for it. He reached to the outer part of the plate, sending

Rockies catcher Tony Wolters connects on his game-winning hit in the 2018 NL wild-card game.

While they waited for their own ballpark to be built, the Rockies called Mile High Stadium home.

the ball back up the middle and into the outfield. Shortstop Trevor Story raced home from third base, and just like that the Rockies were three outs from advancing in the playoffs.

A ROCKY START

Wolters's clutch single was the latest special memory for the Rockies, one of the newest teams in Major League Baseball (MLB). The thought of those moments is what inspired businessmen Mickey Monus and John Antonucci to bring baseball to the Mile High City of Denver in the early 1990s.

As early as 1985, MLB was planning to expand the NL by two teams. At that time, the minor league Denver Zephyrs were celebrating their 100th anniversary. The history of baseball in

Colorado went back even further. The first teams began playing there in the 1860s.

However, going from a minor league city to a major league city wasn't going to be easy. Denver needed a new baseball stadium. In 1990 Denver residents voted to build one.

Monus and Antonucci emerged from among many potential owners to lead the expansion bid. They hosted officials from MLB in March 1991 and arranged a special welcome. The officials were greeted by enthusiastic fans singing "Take Me Out to the Ball Game."

Denver showed its enthusiasm for baseball in other ways too. Its new stadium was still months away from construction. But fans were putting down money for season tickets for a team that did not yet exist. MLB officials were impressed. In July 1991, Denver was chosen along with Miami, Florida, for new teams to begin play in 1993.

NOT THE FIRST ROCKIES

The baseball team wasn't the first Denver-area professional team to use "Rockies" as a nickname. From 1976 to 1982, Colorado had a National Hockey League team also called the Rockies. After the 1981–82 season, the team moved to New Jersey and became the Devils.

READY TO ROCK

When Denver was awarded a franchise, it was the only MLB team in the entire Mountain Time Zone. The defining feature

After the Rockies' initial owners ran into financial trouble, Jerry McMorris stepped in and saved the franchise.

of the region was the Rocky Mountains, so "Rockies" was a perfect fit. The goal, Antonucci said, was that the team would last as long as the mountains.

The Rocky Mountains were the inspiration for the line "purple mountain majesties" in the song "America the Beautiful." So purple was the perfect choice to include in the team's colors. The team also wore black and silver with its pinstripe home uniforms.

Monus and Antonucci ran into financial problems in 1992 and lost control of the team. The Rockies were so short of money that the league threatened to remove the franchise from Denver before it had ever played a game. Another partner in their group of owners, Jerry McMorris, produced the money to save the franchise. The trucking industry millionaire stepped in and became majority owner. He remained in that role until 2005.

The Rockies' new downtown ballpark was not going to be ready by 1993. So the team instead set up at the home of the Broncos, Denver's National Football League (NFL) team. Mile High Stadium seated more than 80,000 fans, far more than any other MLB park. With so many seats available, Colorado smashed the league's all-time attendance record. They drew 4,483,350 fans to Mile High in their first season.

Eric Young's dramatic leadoff home run on April 9, 1993, was one of only three the second baseman hit all season.

Not surprisingly, every seat was full on April 9, 1993, for the first MLB game in Colorado. The Rockies had opened their first season with two road losses to the New York Mets. They returned home to play in front of the biggest crowd ever to see a regular-season MLB game. The festivities included a parade through downtown Denver to welcome baseball to town.

Fans had barely taken their seats when second baseman Eric Young stepped up for the first home plate appearance in Rockies history. And he gave the excited crowd a lasting memory. On a 3–2 count, Young hammered a fastball over the fence in left-center field. The Rockies went on to win 11–4.

It was a fitting start, as games in the Mile High City became known for offense.

DINGER

While building Coors Field, workers made a surprising discovery. There were dinosaur bones in the ground. That inspired the Rockies' mascot, a triceratops named Dinger. The purple dinosaur was "born" during the 1994 season when he "hatched" out of a big egg at a home game.

FLYING HIGH

Like many expansion teams, the Rockies struggled to win games early on. But it wasn't for lack of hitting. The Rockies finished 67–95 in 1993 but scored the fourth-most runs in the NL. Slugging first baseman Andrés Galarraga hit 22 homers and won the batting title with an average of .370.

Players like Galarraga were already great hitters. But they got a little boost by playing in Colorado. Denver sits almost exactly one mile above sea level. The "thin" air at that altitude means less resistance on a flying baseball. It soon became clear that balls simply flew farther in Colorado.

While Rockies hitters may have enjoyed the help, it was the reverse for Colorado's pitchers. They allowed nearly 1,000 runs in 1993, dead last in the NL. It was more of the same in 1994, though Colorado improved to third place.

The Rockies made some big additions for 1995. Colorado signed veteran outfielder Larry Walker before the season. And in April, the team opened its new downtown ballpark, Coors Field. Unlike Mile High Stadium, the new ballpark was made just for baseball. It had the look of classic MLB parks but with all the modern amenities. Fans packed in just as they did at Mile High.

After hitting a career-high 40 home runs in 1995, Rockies right fielder Dante Bichette finished second in NL MVP voting.

More than 47,000 of them were there for Opening Day on April 26 against the Mets. A thrilling back-and-forth game went to 14 innings. In the bottom of the 14th, Colorado outfielder Dante Bichette stepped to the plate with two runners on. On a 2–1 count, he sent a fly ball deep toward left field for the game-winning home run. The walk-off bomb was just the beginning of a magical 1995 season.

ROCKIES

CHAPTER 2

TASTE OF SUCCESS

Dante Bichette's Opening Day heroics started the Rockies off right in 1995. The pitching was still poor, but the Rockies led the NL in home runs and runs scored. In a nod to the team's downtown address, power hitters Bichette, Andrés Galarraga, outfielder Larry Walker, and third baseman Vinny Castilla became known as the "Blake Street Bombers."

On October 1, the Rockies faced the San Francisco Giants at home in the final regular-season game. If the Rockies won, they would make the playoffs. It was another wild game in Denver. And early on it wasn't looking good for the home team.

The Giants raced out to an 8–2 lead by the top of the third inning. But the Rockies started chipping away with their

Vinny Castilla played for six MLB teams but hit 239 of his 320 career home runs with Colorado.

Andrés Galarraga was known as "Big Cat" for his quickness in the field despite a 6-foot-3-inch, 235-pound frame.

big bats. Eric Young and Walker each hit two-run homers in the bottom of the third.

The Rockies threatened again in the fifth. Galarraga smashed a run-scoring double to tie the game. Castilla brought in a run on a ground out and gave the Rockies the lead. Then shortstop Walt Weiss got the crowd roaring with a double down the right-field line. Galarraga scored to put his team up 10–8.

Reliever Curtis Leskanic entered the game in the ninth. As he pitched, he said, his heart was beating hard enough to make his jersey move. But Leskanic looked calm in shutting the Giants down and earning the save.

PLAYOFF BASEBALL

Major league baseball had just come to Denver two years earlier. And playoff baseball had already arrived. No other team in MLB history had made the playoffs earlier than its eighth season. A crowd of 50,040 waited for Game 1 of the NL Division Series (NLDS) against the Atlanta Braves. In the fourth, Castilla hit a two-run bomb to give the Rockies the lead, sending the home crowd into a frenzy. But Leskanic, who had been solid all year, allowed the game-winning homer in the ninth as Atlanta won 5–4.

The Rockies fell behind 3–0 to quiet the crowd in Game 2. They were back on their feet when Walker drilled a three-run homer in the sixth. Then Galarraga ripped a double to drive in a run in the eighth and put the Rockies three outs away from tying the series.

Leskanic got another chance for the save. But he was removed after allowing a leadoff double. His fellow relievers didn't fare much better, as Mike Munoz and Darren Holmes allowed four runs and the Rockies lost 7–4.

The series then went to Atlanta for Games 3 and 4. The Rockies' offense was still clicking. Unfortunately, the pitching was not. The Rockies lost leads of 3–0 and 5–3 in Game 3. But this time, the offensive stars saved the day. Galarraga and Castilla hit back-to-back run-scoring singles in the 10th inning.

When Larry Walker left the Rockies in 2004, he held team records for hits, batting average, home runs, and RBIs.

Pitcher Mark Thompson then shut down Atlanta to secure the first playoff win in Rockies history.

The good feelings didn't last long. Despite a three-run homer in the third inning of Game 4 the next day, Colorado crumbled. Atlanta scored seven unanswered runs on their way to a 10–4 win to close out the best-of-five series.

IT'S CROWDED

Fans packed into Colorado's new ballpark early and often. Starting on June 13, 1995, Colorado sold out 203 straight games. And the Rockies led MLB in attendance every year from 1993 through 1999.

SLUGGING ROCKIES

The Rockies remained a winning team in 1996, finishing 83–79. But in the competitive NL West, that was only good enough for third place. Still, Colorado remained one of baseball's most exciting teams for what their offense could do. That was especially true when playing in Denver.

On September 15, Galarraga launched a three-run home run in the sixth inning against the Houston Astros. That gave the Rockies 628 runs at Coors Field that year. No MLB team had ever scored that many at its home ballpark in a single season. Colorado went on to finish with 658 runs in Denver. That was more than two-thirds of the team's total runs that season.

For the second year in a row, three Rockies hit 40 homers or more in 1997. That included Walker, who hit 49, along with having a .366 average and 130 runs batted in (RBIs). He won the first NL Most Valuable Player (MVP) Award in Rockies history.

Fans got to show their appreciation for Walker in the summer of 1998. Denver hosted the All-Star Game that season. Fans voted in Walker as a starter as he took center stage among baseball's best.

The 1998 season was the first one without the full crew of Blake Street Bombers. Galarraga left after 1997 to sign with Atlanta. But in his position at first base was a promising young slugger named Todd Helton. The rookie would soon become one of Colorado's top stars.

THE QUEST FOR PITCHING

There was no question the Rockies could score enough runs to compete with any team. But the team's problem from the beginning was pitching that could keep enough runs off the board. Even their best was among the worst in baseball. The 1995 Rockies had a team earned-run average (ERA) of 4.97. That mark was last in the NL.

Before the 2001 season, the Rockies went after two of the top free agent pitchers available. On December 4, 2000, the team signed Denny Neagle for $51 million over five years.

Colorado starter Mike Hampton delivers a pitch during the 2002 season.

Just three years earlier he had won 20 games in Atlanta. In Colorado Neagle struggled with injuries and off-field issues. After posting an ERA of 5.57 over three years in Denver, Neagle was released. He never played another MLB game.

Just eight days after signing Neagle, the Rockies shelled out even more money to veteran lefty Mike Hampton. The former Houston Astro had won 22 games with a 2.90 ERA in 1999.

The Rockies gave him $121 million over eight years to play in Denver. At the time, it was the largest contract in baseball history. Hampton never lived up to it. The lefty pitched just 62 games in a Rockies uniform before being traded in 2002.

AFTER THE BOMBERS

The Rockies' pitching solution didn't come on the mound. In 2002 the team installed a humidor at Coors Field. A humidor is a chamber that keeps objects from drying out. Dry baseballs are bouncier and fly farther. The humidor seemed to work. From 1995 to 2001, there were 3.2 home runs per game in Denver. Over the next nine seasons, that number dipped to 2.39.

However, the Rockies weren't scoring as many runs as they used to either. That was in part because the best players had all left. By 2002 only Walker was left from the Blake Street Bombers crew.

But a new bomber had emerged at first base. Helton was in the midst of making five All-Star Games in a row. He could

HAMPTON'S HITS

Although Mike Hampton struggled on the mound in Colorado, he was excellent with the bat. In 143 at-bats over two years, Hampton hit .315 with 10 home runs and 21 RBIs. At one point during the 2001 season, Hampton hit home runs in three straight at-bats.

Todd Helton salutes the fans after a game in 2004.

hit for both average and power. From 1999 to 2004, he had at least 30 homers and hit at least .320 each season.

In 2004 the Rockies brought back Castilla, and he picked up right where he had left off by belting 35 homers. But Walker struggled with injuries and played just 38 games. He was traded in August, leaving as the team's all-time leader in most offensive categories.

The 2004 season also saw the debut season for outfielder Matt Holliday. The Rockies won just 68 games, but the 24-year-old played well. It was a sign that better days were ahead on Blake Street.

CHAPTER 3

ROCKTOBER

Starting in 2005, the Rockies passed up veterans and gave more playing time to their young prospects. That included players like Matt Holliday, who hit .307. Third baseman Garrett Atkins finished fourth in the voting for NL Rookie of the Year that year. Others, like outfielder Brad Hawpe, struggled at times. But the up-and-comers had the time to work through it while the Rockies finished 67–95.

Perhaps the biggest improvement came in the pitching staff. Starter Jeff Francis led all rookies in wins. Fellow starter Aaron Cook showed improvement. And the team found a closer in Brian Flores, who recorded 31 saves.

Matt Holliday was a three-time All-Star in his first stint with the Rockies from 2004–08.

All those players were under the age of 30. But it was 31-year-old first baseman Todd Helton who was by now the cornerstone of the franchise. Helton was an exceptional athlete. In college at the University of Tennessee, he had not just been the star of the baseball team. Helton was also the backup quarterback on the Volunteers' highly ranked football team. The player ahead of him was future NFL legend Peyton Manning. In 2005 Helton once again hit over .300 with 20 home runs. But since joining the Rockies in 1997, he had never made the playoffs. Though the team improved to 76 wins in 2006, time was running out for its star.

A RUDE MEAT-ING

In 2005 Rockies shortstop Clint Barmes suffered one of the most unusual injuries in baseball history. After a hunting trip with teammate Todd Helton, Barmes was carrying a package of deer meat when he fell and broke his collarbone. Barmes missed half the season due to the injury.

A STUNNING COMEBACK

In 2007 the Rockies were the top hitting and fielding team in the NL. Another star was emerging in rookie Troy Tulowitzki. He finished the year with 24 home runs while playing an excellent shortstop. The Rockies' pitching was also the best in team history.

Despite the positives, things didn't look much more promising for the Rockies as the season

The Rockies had four players with at least 20 home runs in 2007, including Garrett Atkins, *left*, and Brad Hawpe, *right*.

was nearing its end. On September 15, a loss dropped the team 6 1/2 games behind the first-place Arizona Diamondbacks and 4 1/2 games out of the NL wild-card lead.

The next day, Colorado trounced the Florida Marlins 13–0. After a day off, the Rockies took both games of a doubleheader against the Los Angeles Dodgers. Game 2 featured a dramatic two-run walk-off homer by Helton to win the game 9–8. Suddenly Colorado couldn't lose. The team ran its streak to 11 games heading into the final weekend's series with the first-place Diamondbacks.

Francis pitched well in the opener. However, the Rockies' winning streak came to an end with a 4–2 setback. Now a division title was no longer possible. But Colorado was still in the race for the wild card as long as it won its last two games.

The Rockies pulled off both victories. When the dust settled, Colorado was tied with the San Diego Padres at 90–72. To decide who went to the playoffs, the teams had to play a one-game tiebreaker.

SLIDING INTO THE PLAYOFFS

The flip of a coin meant the Rockies got to host the play-in game. Colorado had a tough task in facing Padres starter Jake Peavy, who won that year's NL Cy Young Award as the league's best pitcher. But in Denver, both Peavy and Colorado starter Josh Fogg struggled.

The Rockies took a 3–0 lead before a five-run third made it 5–3 San Diego. The Rockies battled back and eventually took a 6–5 lead before San Diego tied it in the eighth. Neither team could get the big hit it needed, and the game went to extra innings.

The visitors broke the tie in the 13th. After a leadoff walk, Rockies pitcher Jorge Julio allowed a two-run home run to San Diego's Scott Hairston. The noisy Rockies crowd suddenly fell silent. They knew that one of the game's top closers was in the

Holliday dives across home plate with the winning run in the 2007 tiebreaker victory over the San Diego Padres.

Padres bullpen. Future Hall of Famer Trevor Hoffman came on to lock down the win for the Padres.

Instead, the Rockies' stars pounced on Hoffman. Kazuo Matsui and Tulowitzki opened with back-to-back doubles to get one run back. Then Holliday hit a triple to knock in Tulowitzki. Once again, the game was tied, and there were still no outs.

Up next was light-hitting infielder Jamey Carroll. He went after Hoffman's first pitch, hitting a fly ball into right field. Holliday broke for home as soon as Brian Giles made the catch. The right-fielder fired a throw home. Holliday dove headfirst, splitting his chin open on the dirt. He was called safe when San Diego catcher Michael Barrett dropped the ball.

Barrett never tagged Holliday. But Holliday also never touched home plate. It didn't matter. Before Barrett could grab

Todd Helton, *left*, and Troy Tulowitzki, *right*, celebrate the final out of the 2007 NLCS.

the ball and tag Holliday, umpire Tim McClelland called him safe. The Rockies won and the team mobbed Holliday. The date was October 1, 2007. "Rocktober" had just begun.

STILL STREAKING

The Rockies needed their miracle run just to reach the playoffs. Some around baseball thought the team had just been lucky. Others wondered if the Rockies had anything left in the tank after the late-season charge. But since May 22, the Rockies' record was the best in the NL. They believed they could play with anyone.

Colorado had to open the NLDS on the road against the Philadelphia Phillies. Francis took the mound for the team's first playoff game in 12 years. He pitched well, allowing just two runs in six innings. Holliday added a home run to help stun the Phillies.

After a 10–5 drubbing of Philadelphia in Game 2, the teams headed back to Denver. Game 3 offered more Rocktober magic. Infielder Jeff Baker, who had hit just .222 in the regular season, broke a 1–1 tie in the bottom of the eighth inning. His single brought home Hawpe with the winning run. With the sweep of Philadelphia, Colorado had won 17 of its last 18 games.

The Diamondbacks were the next hurdle. However, by now the Rockies were seemingly unbeatable. Francis again was at the top of his game in winning Game 1 on the road. Game 2 took 11 innings, but the Rockies once again survived to win 2–1. Back in Denver, the Rockies finished off the sweep. After briefly falling behind in Game 4, Colorado scored six times in the fourth inning. Holliday punctuated the rally with a three-run homer to center field. Colorado held on to win 6–4. The Rockies were on one of the greatest rolls in MLB history, and it was taking them to the World Series.

DON'T STOP THE ROCK

Everything was clicking for the Rockies. They'd won 21 out of their last 22 games. They rolled into the World Series, while the Boston Red Sox had been inconsistent in the playoffs. They had to rally from a 3–1 American League Championship Series deficit to Cleveland.

However, the Rockies' magical run came to an end in a big way in Game 1 at Fenway Park. After having been solid throughout the playoffs, Francis lasted only four innings. He allowed 10 hits and six runs. The veteran Red Sox clubbed the Rockies 13–1.

Helton's RBI groundout put the Rockies up 1–0 early in Game 2. And Rockies pitcher Ubaldo Jiménez matched Red Sox veteran Curt Schilling in a pitcher's duel. Jiménez allowed only two runs, but that was one more than Schilling as the Rockies lost 2–1.

The Rockies hoped to recapture their Rocktober magic upon heading home to Denver. An excited crowd waited for them. But they were silenced in the third inning as Boston scored six runs and eventually won 10–5.

By the start of Game 4, the Rockies' unbeaten playoff run was a distant memory. The Red Sox finished off the sweep. Despite late home runs from Hawpe and Atkins, Boston won 4–3.

Rockies starter Jeff Francis delivers a pitch during Game 1 of the 2007 World Series.

Rocktober came to an end quicker than the Rockies and their fans wanted. But they had gone on one of the most memorable postseason runs in baseball history. And with young talent all over the field, fans in Denver believed the team would be back soon.

CHAPTER 4

CLIMBING NEW PEAKS

On April 17, 2008, the Rockies and San Diego Padres hooked up for another memorable game. This one lasted more than six hours. Troy Tulowitzki finally broke a 1–1 tie with an RBI double in the top of the 22nd inning as Colorado won 2–1.

That was just the first in a season full of thrilling moments for Colorado's young stars. On July 4, the Rockies found themselves trailing at home to the Florida Marlins 13–4 after the top of the fourth. From that point on, the Independence Day fireworks in Denver came early.

By the end of the sixth inning, Matt Holliday, Chris Iannetta, and Garrett Atkins had all homered for Colorado. Outfielder

Troy Tulowitzki won back-to-back Gold Glove Awards at shortstop in 2010 and 2011.

Ryan Spilborghs hit a pair of them. Suddenly the Rockies were only down by a run.

The power surge wasn't nearly over. Florida scored four runs in the seventh. Holliday answered back with a grand slam in the bottom half of the inning. It was still 17–16 Florida in the bottom of the ninth. But Atkins delivered a single to tie the game. Two batters later, Iannetta finished off the greatest comeback in team history. His ground-ball single to left scored Holliday. The rest of the players raced out of the dugout to pounce on both players.

Despite the big moments, the team fell short of the playoffs. Colorado suffered an even bigger loss after the year. Unable to agree on a new contract with Holliday, the Rockies' management traded the star outfielder to the Oakland Athletics.

ANOTHER COMEBACK

The 2009 Rockies started slowly. An 18–28 stumble cost manager Clint Hurdle his job. He was replaced by Jim Tracy on May 29.

The Rockies bounced back to go 21–9 in June. They stayed hot the rest of the way with big performances up and down the lineup. Tulowitzki smashed 32 homers and contended for MVP. Three other Rockies had 20 homers or more.

And rookie outfielder Carlos González, the prize of the Holliday trade, added 13 in just 89 games.

Outfielder Carlos González emerged as a star after coming to Colorado from the Oakland Athletics in the trade for Matt Holliday.

Colorado posted a record of 74–42 after Tracy took over. Despite being 15 1/2 games back in June, the Rockies nearly contended for a division title. All the while, they were in a tight race with the Atlanta Braves for the NL wild-card spot. On September 29, Colorado's lead was down to two games. That night, closer Huston Street blew a save against the Milwaukee Brewers. But Iannetta came to the rescue, hitting a two-run homer in the 11th to strengthen the Rockies' playoff position. They clinched two days later.

The Rockies won a team-record 92 games in 2009. But as the wild card, they again had to go on the road for the NLDS. They would be facing the defending World Series champion Philadelphia Phillies.

Rockies players wait to celebrate with catcher Chris Iannetta, *far right*, after his walk-off home run on September 29, 2009.

Philadelphia ace Cliff Lee shut down the Rockies in a 5–1 Game 1 defeat. The next three games were all decided by one run. Unfortunately for Colorado fans, their Rockies came up short twice. In Game 3, the Phillies broke a 5–5 tie with a run in the top of the ninth inning. Game 4 was even worse. Street gave up three runs on a pair of two-out Philadelphia hits in the ninth. Colorado fans watched a 4–2 lead turn into a season-ending 5–4 loss.

ROCK SLIDE

The 2010 season began with a rare Colorado pitching triumph. In Atlanta, Ubaldo Jiménez tossed the first no-hitter in Rockies

Ubaldo Jiménez delivers a pitch during his no-hitter against the Atlanta Braves in April 2010.

history. That season also saw González burst into stardom as he won the batting title and a Gold Glove Award, while also finishing third in NL MVP voting. But the Rockies slumped to an 83–79 record and out of the playoffs.

Nolan Arenado led the NL in home runs three times and RBIs twice during his eight seasons in Colorado.

Injuries helped continue the slide. By 2012 the Rockies were 64–98, the worst record in team history. Only Jeff Francis, Tulowitzki, and a 38-year-old Todd Helton were left from the famous Rocktober team. Both Francis and Tulowitzki were also battling injuries. It was time to look for new stars.

Rookie third baseman Nolan Arenado made his MLB debut in 2013. A smooth fielder who could hit for power and average, Arenado became one of the key players for the Rockies' future.

A significant member of their past said goodbye after that season. Helton had announced his retirement before the season ended so he could celebrate with Rockies fans. He gave them one final memory, homering in the first at-bat of his final home game. Fans loved Helton for his great play and loyalty, as he played all of his 17 seasons in Rockies purple. He retired holding most of the team's major offensive records.

THE NEXT BIG HOPE

Arenado led the Rockies' turnaround into playoff contenders by 2017. He was helped by outfielder Charlie Blackmon, who was also becoming a star in his fourth full season. The long-haired, bushy-bearded Blackmon was a great contact hitter who won the batting title in 2017. Shortstop Trevor Story had a second-straight 20-homer season. The Rockies earned one of two wild-card spots that year and faced the Diamondbacks in the NL wild-card game, which had been added in 2012 as a regular playoff play-in game. Colorado lost 11–8.

The 2018 Rockies made more team history. Colorado reached the playoffs for a second consecutive season, something it had never done before. It took another midseason turnaround. The Rockies were 38–42 on June 28. But they went 53–30 the rest of the way behind the power combo of Arenado and Story. Colorado nearly won the NL West for the first time, losing in a tiebreaker to the Los Angeles Dodgers. But after unlikely hero Tony Wolters's huge hit in the NL wild-card game, the Rockies won and moved on to the NLDS.

The result was a disappointing three-game sweep against the Brewers. Colorado failed to score in each of the final two games. Big changes were on the way in Denver. González, now 32, left as a free agent. Arenado didn't last much longer. He signed a big contract extension in 2019 but was traded after the 2020 season.

Frustrated after three straight losing seasons, Story left in the spring of 2022 to sign with the Boston Red Sox. The Rockies were again shedding their top veterans to start over with younger players. There was one exception, however. Before the 2022 season, the team signed former MVP third baseman Kris Bryant to a big contract. There was at least one true slugger on the team as Rockies fans dreamed of the next great October run.

FREQUENT FLYERS

The Rockies packed in a lot of travel leading up to the 2018 playoffs. The team played its last game of the regular season in Denver on October 1. The Rockies then went to Los Angeles for the NL West tiebreaker the next day. From there it was on to Chicago for the NL wild-card game against the Cubs. Finally, the Rockies played their fourth game in five days—in four different cities—when they started the NLDS in Milwaukee on October 4.

After watching several stars leave in previous years, the Rockies signed former World Series champion Kris Bryant before the 2022 season to lead the offense.

TIMELINE

1991

Major League Baseball selects Denver and Miami as the sites for new teams to begin play in the 1993 season. The Rockies name and logo are revealed the same day.

1992

Construction gets underway on the team's new downtown ballpark.

1993

Eric Young homers in the first home at-bat in Rockies history, an 11–4 win over the Montreal Expos.

1995

The Rockies become the fastest expansion team to make the playoffs, clinching the NL wild card on October 1.

1997

Larry Walker wins the first NL MVP Award in Rockies history.

2007

After winning 13 of their last 14 games, the Rockies surge from behind to tie the San Diego Padres for the NL wild card. In a tiebreaker game, the Rockies win the wild card 9–8 in 13 innings. The Rockies then sweep two playoff rounds before falling to the Boston Red Sox in the World Series.

2009

After starting 18–28, the Rockies rally to win the wild card before falling 3–1 to the Philadelphia Phillies in the NLDS.

2010

Ubaldo Jiménez pitches the first no-hitter in Rockies history in a game against the Braves in Atlanta.

2013

After a 17-year career with the team, Rockies legend Todd Helton announces his retirement. He holds most of Colorado's major offensive records.

2017

The Rockies win one of two wild-card spots in MLB's expanded playoffs but lose in the NL wild-card game to the Arizona Diamondbacks.

2018

The Rockies make the playoffs in consecutive seasons for the first time ever. After winning the NL wild-card game, the Rockies are swept in the NLDS by the Milwaukee Brewers.

2022

After parting ways with star players Nolan Arenado and Trevor Story in recent years, the Rockies make a splash in signing former NL MVP Kris Bryant.

TEAM FACTS

FRANCHISE HISTORY

Colorado Rockies
(1993–)

KEY PLAYERS

Nolan Arenado (2013–20)
Charlie Blackmon (2011–)
Vinny Castilla (1993–99, 2004, 2006)
Aaron Cook (2002–11)
Andrés Galarraga (1993–97)
Carlos González (2009–18)
Todd Helton (1997–2013)
Matt Holliday (2004–08, 2018)
Ubaldo Jiménez (2006–11)
Trevor Story (2016–21)
Troy Tulowitzki (2006–15)
Larry Walker (1995–2004)

KEY MANAGERS

Don Baylor (1993–98)
Clint Hurdle (2002–09)
Jim Tracy (2009–12)

HOME STADIUMS

Mile High Stadium (1993–94)
Coors Field (1995–)

TEAM TRIVIA

INTERNATIONAL FLAIR

In 1999 the Rockies took part in the first season opener to be played outside the United States or Canada. The Rockies defeated the San Diego Padres 8–2 in Monterrey, Mexico.

FATHER TIME

In 2012 Rockies pitcher Jamie Moyer became the oldest pitcher in MLB history to record a win. The 49-year-old actually had two wins that year, his final season in the big leagues.

WHAT'S NEW IS OLD

While the Rockies are one of MLB's youngest teams, Coors Field is the third-oldest stadium in the NL. Only Chicago's Wrigley Field (1914) and Los Angeles's Dodger Stadium (1962) are older than the park that opened in 1995.

QUITE A DEBUT

On August 23, 2001, Rockies pitcher Jason Jennings made history during his MLB debut. Jennings tossed a five-hit shutout of the New York Mets, striking out eight batters. Even better, he led off the ninth inning with a solo home run. No MLB player had ever debuted with both a pitching shutout and a home run before Jennings did it.

GLOSSARY

ace

A team's best starting pitcher.

batter's box

The marked area on either side of home plate where the batter stands to hit.

changeup

A pitch that looks like a fastball but is thrown much more slowly to deceive the hitter.

closer

A pitcher who comes in at the end of the game to secure a win for his team.

debut

First appearance.

expansion

The addition of new teams to increase the size of a league.

free agent

A player whose rights are not owned by any team.

no-hitter

A complete game in which a pitcher does not allow any hits.

rookie

A professional athlete in his or her first year of competition.

veteran

A player who has played many years.

MORE INFORMATION

BOOKS

Gitlin, Marty. *Baseball: Underdog Stories*. Minneapolis, MN: Abdo Publishing, 2019.

Hustad, Douglas. *Innovations in Baseball*. Minneapolis, MN: Abdo Publishing, 2021.

Mitchell, Bo. *Ultimate MLB Road Trip*. Minneapolis, MN: Abdo Publishing, 2019.

ONLINE RESOURCES

To learn more about the Colorado Rockies, please visit **abdobooklinks.com** or scan this QR code. These links are routinely monitored and updated to provide the most current information available.

INDEX

ABOUT THE AUTHOR

Anthony K. Hewson is a freelance writer originally from San Diego. He and his wife now live in the San Francisco Bay Area with their two dogs.